Starting Your Own Venture Investment Fund

- A How to Guide -

By Kevin J. Moore

Whether you work in venture capital or some other industry, this book offers a step-by-step guide on how you can get started raising, managing, and investing from your own investment fund.

To Rachel, Isaac, and Taylor

STARTING YOUR OWN VENTURE INVESTMENT FUND

A How to Guide

ISBN-13: 978-0-9998171-0-0

ISBN-10: 0-9998171-0-8

Contents

Introduction

My journey into venture started in engineering. That's right – engineering. Although I received my degree in engineering, I became interested in investing and finance shortly after graduating. After transitioning out of engineering and working in a series of roles with various financial firms, I took my first step into venture with a firm called i2E (Innovation to Enterprise). i2E primarily made investments into early-stage, startup technology and life science companies. My role at the organization involved working closely with companies on business strategy, marketing, financial modeling, business valuation, and raising capital. I also managed and led i2E's angel investment group, which co-invested with i2E into i2E portfolio companies.

I thoroughly enjoyed the work. It was fun. But I later came to realize that angel investors were better off if they could invest collectively in a fund versus investing individually on a deal-by-deal basis. Typically, the first investors in a startup are friends and family; after that, it's Angel Investors. Angel investing is risky because investors are investing at the seed-stage in the life of a company. Other than what an entrepreneur says to be true, there really isn't much evidence to prove a seed-stage startup company will work.

Having conducted mountains of research underscoring the risks of angel investing, I felt there was sufficient data to suggest that investing from a fund into early-stage companies would have a positive impact on performance. So, I proposed to management that we create our own private, early-stage angel investment fund. Fortunately, starting a fund was top-of-mind for the organization so they gave me the green light to get it going.

To be frank, I had very minimal knowledge on how to start an investment fund. I had a general sense of how funds worked based on my past experience in the financial sector and from talking to people who were already operating funds.

From that point forward, my colleagues and I spent the next 18 months going step-by-step through the process of starting and raising a venture fund. The most challenging part of starting the fund was not having a simple, yet comprehensive outline to guide us through the initial steps of the process. I cold called and scheduled meetings with fund managers all over the country; read numerous books and articles; and even got advice from experienced investors.

After going through the lengthy process of gathering information and piecing it all together, I thought to myself that someone should consolidate all the information I gathered and put it into one place. Hence, the reason for this book.

Have you ever found yourself in a similar situation? Wanting or needing to start a fund, but not knowing where to start? With the steps outlined in this book, you can learn the basics of what it takes to raise and operate a venture investment fund. Although your situation will likely be different from mine, the process for researching, raising, and operating a fund is generally the same. My hope is that this book will help you avoid the mistakes and pitfalls I made so you can get off to a fast start.

1 Fund Research

The first step in the process is conducting research. Conducting proper research is critical to understanding the basics of how a fund works and will help you learn the ins-and-outs of the venture industry. Performing research also helps with developing your fund strategy and gathering perspectives from others in the industry who are already doing what you want to do.

The other, and probably far greater, reason for performing research is to gain awareness about the difficulties of successfully raising and operating a venture fund. In the beginning of most new endeavors, there is usually a heightened sense of excitement about how fun it will be and how everything will be smooth sailing. There is absolutely nothing wrong with being excited about the possibility of running your own fund. The truth is, running a fund *is* fun and not many people get to do it. However, it's prudent to temper your enthusiasm by understanding the not so fun aspects as well. Try to fully embrace the process of research so that you have a well-rounded understanding of both the good and bad aspects of running a venture fund.

Assessing Your Network

To begin the research process, the first thing I did was create a list of fund managers I personally knew within my network. Next, I created a separate list of fund managers who I did not personally know but wanted to talk to at some point. The importance of meeting with people you do not know is to gain additional perspectives on how they do things and for obtaining more direct and unbiased advice. More often than not, those within your immediate network may sugar coat some of the more challenging aspects of operating a fund. On the other hand, those who do not know you are far less likely to paint a rosy picture. In my personal experience, I found the calls with people outside of my network to be much more beneficial, especially when I was asking questions about the not-so-fun side of fund management.

The perspectives of those within and outside your network will be different, but that's a good thing. I implore you to make the cold calls and send emails to the fund managers you personally do not know. Skipping these calls is cheating the process and you'll be missing out on information and feedback that you desperately need in the early stage of formation.

The first few fund managers I spoke with were angel group managers like me who had transitioned from a network model to a pooled investment model. A network model is a group of investors who invest into the same company, but each investor decides individually how much he or she wants to invest. Most angel managers would agree that one of the challenges of investing in a network model is uncertainty around having an adequate number of investors to fully fund a company's investment round. Another challenge for angel investors is achieving an adequate level of diversification in their personal investment portfolio. In my experience, I have seen how some angel investors find it difficult at times to adhere to an investment strategy that has less to do with picking "winners" and more to do with following a disciplined investment strategy.

Due Diligence Calls

As you make due diligence calls, it's important to approach each conversation with a purpose. Keep meetings to thirty minutes or less and maintain an open mind as you learn new ideas. There is no industry standard for the perfect fund structure, so embrace the fact that there will be differences in structure from fund to fund.

As you begin setting up calls, approach each conversation with a confident mindset. All fund managers were once at a point in their careers where they were just starting out and didn't fully understand how things worked. What you'll find is that the majority of fund managers are nice people and are very open to sharing what they've learned in their careers.

The venture industry is small and most people in the business have themselves received advice and direction from someone more experienced at some point or another. So, don't be bashful – ask as many questions as you need. Even though it's a competitive industry, most people are willing to help as a way of giving back.

Developing Your Phone Script

When you begin making phone calls I recommend using a script. Using a script is especially helpful if you're calling someone for the first time. You can create your own script, or you can use the one I made when I first started making calls. A phone script should be more of a guide than something you read verbatim. It should be used to keep you focused and steady. Practice your script a few times prior to your calls so you sound natural, calm, and confident. See the script I used below:

> *"Hi [Name] – My name is [Name] and I am the [Title] in [Any town, USA]. I'm in the process of researching and gathering information about how to start a fund, so I thought I'd reach out to see if you had time in the next couple of weeks to share some advice on that process. Would you have time for a phone call in the next week or two?"*

Your script can be delivered via phone or email. I prefer making the first contact by phone because you get an immediate "yes, no, or maybe" response. **Always try for the phone call first**. If the person doesn't answer, leave a message. Then the next day if you haven't heard back, send a follow-up email. What matters most is delivering the message and getting on the person's radar to eventually get the meeting set up.

Interview Questions

Once you have a few meetings set up, you need to have prepared questions to ask. Remember, the purpose of these meetings isn't to immediately dive into all of the nitty-gritty details of fund management. Instead, the purpose should be to obtain the type of information you cannot obtain from reading a text book. Such questions include:

1. Tell me about the thought process you went through when starting your fund?
2. Did you find it difficult to decide on the right structure?
3. How did you first go about educating investors and getting buy-in about the concept?
4. What were some of the mistakes you made in the beginning?
5. Can you tell me about your process for targeting investors?

6. How did you deal with pushback from peers and investors when you were first starting out?

7. What kind of pushback did you most commonly receive?

8. Can you tell me a little bit about how you developed your investment thesis?

The information you'll collect from personal interviews is invaluable. There are several mechanical aspects of operating a fund, but most of that stuff you can learn from reading books or online sources. Spending time talking with people who successfully started a fund is far better than spending a week reading a book on how to do it (*except this book of course*). If you can set up two or three of these meetings per week, it will exponentially increase your learning curve.

I spent six months collecting data and talking with 24 different fund managers prior to approaching investors about the fund we were raising. I'm not implying it will take you as long as it took me, but the most important thing to remember at this stage is ***not to rush the research process***. Unless you have a set deadline for starting your fund, take as much time as you need to learn what you need to know. It's better to start your fund a little later and do it successfully than to start it too early and have to backtrack and start over.

Action Items

1. Spend a few minutes writing your phone script. Having a script gives you confidence and clarity as you approach each phone call. Keep your script succinct.
2. Practice your script prior to making phone calls to prevent sounding robotic. A key part of feeling confident on the phone is deliberate practice beforehand.
3. Draft a set of questions you'd like to ask each fund manager during your calls. It's good to ask the same set of questions each time so

you can track the differences in responses from conversation to conversation and so you don't have to think of new questions for every call.

4. Set a goal for the number of conversations you'd like to have. I recommend having a minimum of 20 unique conversations with fund managers both from inside and outside of your immediate network.

2 Developing a Fund Thesis

The Webster Dictionary defines a thesis as "a proposition stated or put forward for consideration, especially one to be discussed and proved to be maintained against objections." Okay, that makes sense. But what then is an *investment* thesis? An investment thesis is a hypothesis that describes how or why there is an existing or future opportunity in a particular market suitable for producing a positive investment return.

If you've started step four of the Action Items at the end of Chapter One, you've likely spoken with a handful of fund managers and heard a few different thesis statements you can build on. You never want to plagiarize another person's thesis statement - that's unprofessional. However, there is nothing wrong with studying different theses to get a sense for how they're put together and to categorize which ones you think are good and which ones you think are great.

Thesis Development

The need to develop a compelling, yet concise thesis statement is paramount, as it is usually the first piece of information investors will read about your fund. A good thesis statement is similar to having attractive landscaping on a new house. If you're selling a house and the landscaping out front is visually appealing, buyers are more likely to go inside to check it out. For example, a few years ago, my friend and I decided to flip a house. We did a great job fixing up the interior of the home, but we woefully neglected the landscaping. We eventually sold the house, but early in the cycle we missed out on a lot of qualified buyers because as good as the house was on the inside, we failed to attract buyers because the house was visually unappealing on the outside. The same goes for your thesis. If your thesis is unappealing, investors will be less enthused to dive deeper into the details of your fund. As a side note, real estate is not my forte so if you're starting a real estate investment fund please don't ask me for investment advice!

A strong thesis is one that is immediately easy to understand and can be communicated in a sentence or two. In fact, anytime I'm working on a thesis statement I always ask my nine-year-old son if he can understand at a high level what I'm talking about. I don't expect him to give me feedback on how to construct my thesis, but he serves as a good test subject for whether or not the thesis statement is direct, clear, and simple.

Listed below are a few examples of what I consider strong thesis statements:

> **#1** – In fifteen years cashiers will be obsolete and retailers will rely on machines to perform the same function for a fraction of the cost.

#2 – Bitcoin usage will become ubiquitous eliminating the need for cash for purchasing products online.

#3 – Autonomous vehicles are safer than human drivers.

I want you to notice that each of these statements are clear, direct, and easily understood. Whether they are true or not is another topic. Your thesis statement is your own, and the overall goal is to get other people to buy into it. Getting buy-in is not always easy, but it is doable.

Let's now take a look at few poor thesis statements:

#1 - Our product helps address the low recycle rate of plastic bottles in the United States.

#2 - Drivers use a lot of fuel traveling to work each day and are generally in a rush.

#3 - My fund will invest in companies that develop artificial intelligence software.

Your thesis may seem more compelling to investors if you have an investment strategy that focuses on a particular industry vertical, like technology or healthcare. There's nothing wrong with being a generalist in a particular vertical, but usually the better venture firms tend to stick to one vertical or another. There are a few venture firms who've successfully invested across multiple verticals, but it is not widely common. Specialists are usually borne by having direct experience within a certain vertical and will usually attract entrepreneurs seeking their expertise. If you view yourself as a specialist in a particular area, great. The next step will be convincing investors that you are. More on that later.

Action Items

1. Spend a few minutes drafting your thesis statement. It is helpful to write your thesis in a few different formats until you find the best flow.

2. Test your thesis statement with a stranger to determine if it's immediately easy to understand. If you have young children, try reading it to them. Children can often be the most honest critics!

3 Creating Marketing Materials

In this chapter, we're going to dig into the details of formalizing your executive summary and creating your presentation deck. Preparing marketing materials is essential to the overall process of starting your fund so you'll want to pay close attention to the details. If you don't feel confident in your creative skills, don't worry. Focus on the content; you can always find someone else to help with the design.

Making an Executive Summary

There are several ways you can organize your executive summary, but it's best to include (at a minimum) the following sections: Fund Objectives, (Legal) Structure, Fund Specifics, Investment Strategy, Investment Criteria, Investment Process Overview, Management Team, and Disclaimers.

Fund Objective

The fund objectives section provides a high-level overview of what you intend to accomplish in the fund. This is a great area to add color to your thesis and discuss it in more detail. You might also state your reasons for why now is the right time for your fund and what companies will benefit the most from its creation. It doesn't need to be overly complicated – keep it simple.

Legal Structure

Most venture capital funds are established as limited partnerships. A limited partnership must have at least one general partner and one limited partner (LP). The general partner (GP) is responsible for managing the fund and selecting investment opportunities for the fund. In most cases, the GP is a separate legal entity set up as an LLC. Find an experienced securities attorney to help with the legal work. Do not do it yourself.

Fund Specifics

In this area of the executive summary you need to outline the key specifics of the fund. Start by describing the target fund size and the number of years until the fund terminates. In venture, it is standard to have a fund life of ten years, but in some cases, that can be slightly shorter (seven to eight years) or longer (twelve to fifteen years) depending on the type of fund it is. For most early stage funds, ten years is the standard as that usually allows enough time for companies to mature and be liquidated in a timely manner. You'll also want to describe the parameters for extending the life of the fund beyond the maturity date if more time is needed for companies to mature. Extensions are typically one year and have limits on the number of times they can be exercised.

Distribution Strategy

Distributing funds upon the liquidation of portfolio investments is at the full discretion of the general partner (GP). In most funds, there is a recycle provision that states the GP can reinvest fund profits back into the fund instead of immediately distributing them to limited partners. Some funds might establish a performance hurdle-rate, which is a minimum return to LPs before the GP shares in the profits. For most venture capital funds, the hurdle rate is met when 100% of contributed capital is returned to limited partners. After which, the GP/LP split is triggered (more on that later).

Limited Partner Units

Limited partner units are shares that you have for sale in your fund. You'll want to provide details on how many units you are offering for purchase as well as the offering price per unit. Keep in mind that since your fund is considered a private investment fund, you are limited to a maximum of ninety-nine accredited investors in the fund. According to the Securities and Exchange Commission, an accredited investor, in the context of a natural person, includes anyone who earned income that exceeded $200,000 (or $300,000 together with a spouse) in each of the prior two years, and reasonably expects the same for the current year, OR has a net worth over $1 Million, either alone or together with a spouse (excluding the value of the person's primary residence). Ask your attorney for guidance in this area because you do not want to permit unqualified/unaccredited investors in your fund.

Fee Structure

A two-percent, annual management fee is very common in venture and should not be an issue with most investors. There are some VCs who charge a 2.5% annual management fee, but this is the exception, not the norm (at least for now). If this is your first fund, you might consider giving early investors and anchor LPs (*Anchor LPs are your largest, initial investors that help give credibility to you and your fund*) a discount on the annual management fee as an incentive for early participation. A twenty-five to fifty basis point discount rate can make a big difference in the long-run for an investor especially if they make a sizable commitment to your fund. In most cases, <u>the annual management fee is charged on committed capital</u>, and less often, on invested capital. There has been some debate amongst LPs on which fee structure is most fair, but for the most part LPs are accustomed to paying the fee on committed capital.

Compensation Structure

Investment profits can be split a variety of ways, but they are customarily split eighty percent to LPs and twenty percent to the GP. This concept is fairly straightforward and doesn't warrant much explanation. One thing worth mentioning, however, is while the 80/20 split is very common, it is not mandatory. Your split can be set at whatever you want such as 75/25, 85/15, or even 90/10. Amongst these, a 75/25 is probably the most common alternative to using an 80/20 split. As stated previously, the LP/GP split normally will not activate until 100% of contributed capital has been returned to LPs. In some cases, if the GP returns more than 100% to LPs within a predetermined, shorter timeframe, the GP can increase the LP/GP split in their favor. For example, if 110% of capital is returned within one year the LP/GP split may change from 80/20 to 75/25. As you work through the process of structuring your LP/GP split, look at several examples and design a compensation structure that makes sense for you and your investor base.

Initial Deposit

It is not unusual for an early stage, micro VC fund (defined as a fund with less than $50M in assets) to ask its investors to make an upfront, initial deposit to the fund. The amount of the initial deposit can be calculated as a certain percent of an investor's total commitment. When we officially started our first fund, the initial deposit we required from investors was fifteen percent. For a small fund, initial deposits are helpful as they help to subsidize the initial startup costs of the fund. Use extreme prudence in how you handle all funds coming into the fund because the goal is to direct as much of an LP's dollars toward investing in companies, not just for paying legal and accounting fees or superfluous overhead costs.

Many venture funds might have what is called a "Dry Close." A dry close is when an investor makes a commitment to invest in a fund but is not required to fund their commitment at the moment the initial closing documents are signed and submitted. In a dry close, it is understood that the fund manager will request capital at a later date, usually after she has identified the first investment for the fund.

Investment Strategy

The fund's investment strategy should be simple and straightforward. Attempts to make it more complicated than it really is will only confuse you and your investors. Be sure to describe the timeframe with which you intend to deploy capital (usually three to six years) and how much capital you intend to reserve for follow-on investments. You should have an idea of the number of companies you'd like to invest in. The total number of companies to add to a portfolio varies, but it is usually a function of fund size and the maximum investment per company. For example, seed-stage investments require less upfront capital, so if you intend to invest in twenty seed-stage companies at $250K per company, your fund size will likely be in the range of $6 to $7M. You first thought may be that 20 x $250K is only $5M. However, having a fund size slightly larger than $5M is necessary to account for management fees and follow-on investments. You can also specify a desired investment size per company, an investment valuation limit, as well as what vertical(s) you intend to target for investment.

Management Team

When introducing your management team there's no need to write an autobiography. Keep your bios simple by listing any and all relevant past operational experience, educational background, and past investment experience you have. Although it's not required, I personally think it's helpful to have at least two general partners managing a fund. For larger venture capital funds there is usually one general partner for every $50 million of assets under management. If your fund is sub $50M, then it may not make sense to have two GPs right off the bat due to fund economics.

Operating a fund is hard and it is often easier when a second person is involved. When you're first starting out, you might consider adding an operating partner as opposed to a second general partner. If you have an advisory team, you should also list their names and backgrounds in this section as well. Showing the depth of your team enhances the professional look and feel of your fund to investors.

Disclaimers

It's important to work with your attorney to include at the end of your executive summary a disclaimer that states the materials you distribute to potential investors does not constitute an offer to solicit, and that the materials are provided for informational purposes only.

Pitch Deck

A pitch deck is a presentation that gives your audience an overview of your organization. Pitch decks can vary in content and length, but at a minimum, your pitch deck should contain the following sections:

- Team overview
- Market overview
- Fund thesis
- Performance data
- Summary of strengths
- Investment strategy
- Fund specifics (fees, carry, etc.)

There are a multitude of pitch deck examples on the web so I'm not going to spend a great amount of time explaining how to build one. Just make sure your pitch deck is thoughtfully organized, visually interesting, and can be presented in a conversational and professional manner.

Action Items

1. Find five sample executive summaries that you like and study the layout, content, and design.

2. Create an outline for what sections you'd like to include in your executive summary and start adding content.

3. Share your executive summary with someone you respect and ask for feedback. The executive summary is the first document potential investors are likely to see so make every effort to make sure it's perfect before you start marketing.

4. Find a few pitch decks to study and use them as example for how to construct yours so you're not starting from scratch. There's no sense in recreating the wheel when there are proven formats that work.

4 Prospecting

Constructing a prospect list is a necessary and crucial step in the fund formation process. The process is straightforward and starts with sitting down with your team and making a list of every qualified person or entity you think would be interested in learning about your fund. One of the benefits of having a partner is combining each other's network to increase the pool of prospects.

For first-time funds, it is a more efficient use of time to target investors that are open to investing in new fund managers and aren't going to have as much of an issue with a lack of performance history. Such investors include family offices, high net worth individuals (HNI), and foundations. These types of investors sometimes invest for reasons other than just achieving a "return." This by no means implies they are less sophisticated investors; it just means they've allocated a portion of their portfolios for investing in newer, emerging opportunities. Larger, institutional investors (like a pension fund), on the other hand, are less likely to consider an investment into a newer, unproven fund for the following reasons:

1. No prior performance

    Institutional investors most always have desired minimum, expected investment return requirements. If there is no previous performance to speak of it becomes very difficult to assess a manager's potential ability to produce a desired return. However, there are exceptions. Some institutional investors seek out first-time managers through their emerging manager programs, such as K.W. Kellogg Foundation or New York State Common Retirement fund [1]."

While institutions like this do exist, it's better in the beginning stages to target them sparingly.

2. The fund may be too small

    a. In most cases, institutional investors do not like to be more than a certain percent of any one fund due to concentration limits (usually < 20%). In addition, if the investment is too small, the administrative work to monitor an investment that will not make a real impact on the portfolio is not worth the effort.

For example, I'm on the board of trustees for the Oklahoma Teacher's Retirement System Pension Fund (OTRS), a $16 billion pension fund. OTRS has roughly five-percent allocated to alternative investments, which includes private equity, master limited partnerships, and venture capital. When we were raising our first fund at i2E, it was only $3 million, which pales in comparison to the $800

million allocation established at OTRS. Our fund
would have been a mere 0.375 percent investment of
OTRS's total portfolio allocation into alternatives,
and just 0.02 percent of their overall portfolio. An
investment into our fund would have been
pathetically small. The overall message here is to
not waste your time prospecting with larger,
institutional investors unless you know it's a sure
bet. Otherwise, it's just not a good use of your time.

As you build out your prospect list,
remember that all of your investors must be
accredited. One of the last things you want to do is
target individuals who legally cannot participate in
your offering. Do not mass distribute marketing
materials (electronically or printed) as a way to
advertise your offering. Doing so is a violation of
securities law and could lead to the eventual
shutdown of your fund.

Placement Agents

One way you can scale your marketing efforts is to
work with a placement agent or an investment

consultant. Placement agents are good at building relationships with qualified investors and can help you find and place new investors into your fund. They are usually compensated via a success fee (i.e. a percent) on the amount of assets they place for you and often are often paid after you've successfully closed your fund. The placement fee and structure and timing of payment can vary, but the fee is usually in the range of 2 to 3 percent.

Investment Consultants

Investment consultants are similar to financial advisors in that they manage a client's finances and can make recommendations for new investments into client portfolios. In some cases, investment consultants have full discretionary control of a client's assets and can independently choose to invest in new opportunities without client approval. Investment consultants are generally easy to find with a quick google search, but they can sometime be difficult to get in touch with. If you think you may want to market to investment consultants, you'll need to begin contacting them sooner in the fundraising process than later. There is often a long lead time and these days consultants have many different funds to choose from.

Action Items

1. Create a list of potential investors. I recommend categorizing each investor as a high net worth individual, foundation, corporation, or family office.

2. Include the name of the contact person, date of initial contact, follow-up date, and who on your team provided the lead for that contact.

3. You should also keep a record of any marketing materials you leave with potential investors. This may seem excessive, but it's best to have strong records just in case you're ever accused of marketing to unqualified or unaccredited investors.

5 Getting Investor Buy-In

Getting buy-in early on in the fundraising process is important. "Buy-in" in this sense is "agreement." First, it helps with building self-confidence in yourself that people trust you with their money and it helps to build credibility with future investors. Establishing credibility can also be achieved by listing prior performance. On a manager-by-manager basis, performance is measured by a term called attribution. Attribution is a measure of financial performance attributed to an individual manager from investments they've made in the past. If you've never had the sole responsibility of managing a fund and you have a cloudy attribution history, you should spend some time thinking through the ways you contributed to a fund or a company's success and attempt to present that information in a quantifiable manner. For example, if you were an observer on a company's board and made meaningful contributions to that company's success, you should count that towards your attribution.

As you approach investors you'll want to have attribution data front and center. You'll especially want to show this list to your Anchor Investors. Anchor Investors are defined as your largest and most influential investors. They are able to write big checks and are comfortable with publicly endorsing your fund. Mentioning a few prominent names of investors who have invested in your fund can be tremendously advantageous when talking to investors outside of your immediate network. Some investors prefer anonymity and will not want you to publicly advertise their involvement. However, securing Anchor Investors who *are* comfortable publicly endorsing you is always helpful for gathering momentum during the fundraising process.

Preparing for Meetings

When you have a meeting with a potential investor always know in advance how you plan to mentally pace yourself through the meeting. Mental pacing helps you to keep on task and stay within the allotted time for your presentation. Pacing also involves knowing the materials you plan to use during the meeting. If the meeting is with someone in your network that you have a great degree of trust and history with, then using just an executive summary should suffice. On the contrary, if the meeting is with someone whom you are meeting with for the first time, then it's best to take them through the majority of your pitch deck to properly introduce them to who you are and what you aim to accomplish with your fund. Whenever I am in a meeting with a potential investor I like to use the pitch deck to highlight important points and to guide me and the investor through the conversation. In my experience, I've noticed that more experienced investors are usually okay not

going page-by-page through an entire pitch deck
and instead prefer to talk through things through at
a high-level. Whatever situation you may
encounter, the objective of every meeting is to
highlight the key points and allow the investor to
fill in the blanks using the detailed information in
your pitch deck. Use your judgment to determine
how to proceed through each meeting. Or, you can
simply ask up front what the investor is hoping to
cover in the meeting. Asking an investor what she
wants to cover demonstrates that you respect the
investors time and it shifts the focus of the meeting
form you to her.

As you progress through your meetings, pay
careful attention to the investor's buying cues.
Buying cues come in many flavors so take note of
both the good and bad ones. Investors usually never
make a commitment to invest at an in-person
meeting because they'll need to think about it or run
it by their team first. If you're lucky enough to get a
soft commitment at an in-person meeting, then

more power to you. It goes without saying that the more soft commitments you have, the better chance you'll have in reaching your fundraising goal.

Starting out, you'll want to approach the largest investors on your prospect list first. If you're still early in the fundraising process, you may still be at a point where you haven't officially launched your fund. This is perfectly fine. Pre-fundraising meetings are good for getting a general sense for how responsive the market will be to your fund once it officially launches. Use this soft marketing period to collect feedback and to determine whether or not you have enough early adopters to get your fund off the ground. If perhaps after (or during) the pre-fundraising/soft marketing phase you realize that the majority of the larger investors you spoke with aren't keen on your fund or on you as a manager, you can either take the feedback and fix the issues, postpone the fund, or abandon the fund altogether.

Dealing with Pushback

Whether this is your first fund or your tenth, you are likely to experience some form of pushback when pitching to investors. Pushback is neither good nor bad – it's just a part of the process and must be anticipated. If you've thoroughly prepared in advance for each meeting, you're less likely to be thrown off your game when fielding pushback from investors.

One of the most common questions you should be prepared to answer is "What is your past performance?" If you have past performance data, it should be clearly detailed in your pitch deck. If you don't have past performance data directly attributable to you, then you should describe your attribution in relation to those particular investments. As previously mentioned, if you sourced and invested in a company that ended up having a successful exit, you should talk about that. Or, if you have a personal investment portfolio that has performed well, that should also be discussed.

Lastly, if you were an operator of a successful 3
company, that experience should be listed.

In addition to listing your own experience, it is helpful to research other funds with a similar thesis and structure, primarily for comparison and benchmarking purposes (*Preqin and Cambridge Associates provide benchmarking data for venture and private equity funds*). It may be difficult to collect a large quantity of specific investment *return* data because for newer, smaller funds the data may not exist yet. In fact, the increase in the number of Micro-VCs (VC funds with total assets under management of $50 million) has risen rapidly in the last five years. And because most of these funds are investing in very early-stage deals, many are still at the bottom of the J-curve having only posted a few (if any) profitable exits. Nevertheless, you can still use this and other examples to highlight the growth in Micro-VCs and how they are filling a void in helping early-stage companies obtain the financing they need. According to MatterMark, more potential LPs are looking at the micro-VC category as a way to get exposure to venture capital [1]. Deal flow for smaller funds has increased rapidly because the growth in the number of entrepreneurs starting companies has significantly increased, partly due to the lower capital requirements and the inexpensive nature of marketing through social media platforms. Per Cambridge Associates, the declining costs of building technology companies has enabled technology entrepreneurship to expand rapidly. The pace of innovation continues to accelerate, and innovative startups are increasingly addressing global markets from the moment they begin selling [2].

Discussing Metrics that Matter

There are three main performance metrics in venture capital that matter the most: Net Internal Rate of Return (Net IRR), Total Value to Paid in Capital (TVPI), and Distributions to Paid in Capital (DPI). Net IRR measures the performance (i.e. fund distributions and increase or decrease in value of underlying companies) over time of a fund's portfolio, <u>after management fee</u>s. TVPI measures the <u>total value of a fund's holdings plus</u> <u>distributions as compared to total paid in capital.</u> TVPI is also useful metric for determining how much a portfolio's intrinsic value has increased in value above the original investment amount. Lastly, DPI measures total distributions paid to investors compared to total paid in capital. <u>For many</u> <u>investors, DPI is the most important metric because</u> it measures the true <u>cash-on-cash multiple investors</u> <u>have received from an investment</u>. In a venture capital fund (or any fund for that matter)<u>, a DPI</u> <u>greater than or equal to 1.0x is desired.</u> More detailed definitions of these terms will be explained later in the book.

Unquantifiable Metrics That Matter

When talking about performance metrics, investors should also know what your performance-drivers are. Performance <u>Drivers are the key traits or</u> <u>characteristics about your investment strategy that</u>

drive investment performance. It's easy to display performance numbers, but numbers alone don't always tell the whole story, especially when investing in venture capital. It is helpful for investors to know (1) your process for finding and maintaining good, quality deal flow; (2) your pricing strategy for when and how you'll invest; (3) what qualities you look for in entrepreneurs; (4) what you look for in co-investment partners; (5) your philosophy on taking board seats. Your performance drivers need to be well thought out and carefully articulated. However, if this is your first fund your performance drivers will likely change over time as you gain experience and experiment with what works and what doesn't work.

Similar to real estate, the geographic location of a venture capital firm can play a role in the availability of good deals. Ideal locales include areas with growing business districts, prominent universities, and a large and diverse consumer base.

In areas such as these, you also find the business community is made up of successful entrepreneurs who are now themselves investing in startups. There are also universities with programs designed to encourage and teach students what it takes to build a successful company. In fact, there are many universities that now offer courses about venture capital taught by venture capitalists, which is tremendously helpful. Areas with a large and diverse consumer base are great for testing new and innovative ideas. However, given that so many companies operate online, testing new ideas isn't as difficult as it used to be. As stated previously, startups are increasingly addressing global markets from the moment they open for business.

Regardless of the industry, having a good reputation in business is critical. For VC firms, reputation is everything, especially as it relates to attracting high-quality entrepreneurs and co-investing with other venture firms. It is quite common for experienced entrepreneurs to spend time researching a venture capitalist's background before ever making contact with the firm. If the firm in question has a reputation for being harsh to entrepreneurs by demeaning them in meetings or offering unfriendly deal terms, that firm is likely to miss out on good opportunities. On the other hand, if the firm has a reputation for helping entrepreneurs with strategy, product development, building strong management teams, and offering balanced deal terms, that firm is likely to attract and have first dibs on better opportunities.

Deal Flow

While a firm's geography and reputation are important, they do not matter as much if there's not a consistent focus on deal curation. Active deal curation involves engaging in activities that reinforce a VC's expertise and position in a particular industry such that they attract entrepreneurs. Such activities include hosting open-houses to allow entrepreneurs to meet members of the firm and other fellow entrepreneurs; publishing

articles or <u>blogs about strategy, business</u> [2]
<u>development, and trends in technology; speaking at</u>
[3] <u>tradeshows and conferences</u> and <u>positioning one's</u>
[4] <u>self as an expert in a particular area</u>. For example,
each month Josh Breinlinger at Jackson Square
Ventures selects an interesting book on business or
some other topic and mails it out to the firm's
entrepreneurs and limited partners. He later invites
the book recipients to the firm's office for a fireside
chat with the author of the book. It's a creative
approach for adding value that has worked well for
his firm. This is one example of how a VC firm can
enrich the entrepreneurial community and reinforce
its standing and reputation at the same time.

At the end of the day, the objective for every
investor is to make a profit on their investment. And
because it takes so long to reap the rewards of
investing in venture capital, it's important that VC
firms focus their efforts on securing good
companies to invest in on a consistent basis. There is
a high propensity for failure with early-stage

companies and smart VCs make every effort to invest in the best companies, with the best teams, every single time, with no exceptions. Investing in this manner doesn't guarantee every investment is going to be profitable, but VC firms that can are usually the ones who are consistently top-performers.

Getting investor buy-in is a fairly straightforward concept, but it's not easy and it takes time. Understandably, time is your enemy when raising a fund because you usually aren't being paid during the fundraising process. While not making money is not fun, falling short of your fundraising goal is even less so. However, getting investor buy-in early on will help you accelerate the fundraising process so don't underestimate the importance of this step.

Action Items

Spend a few moments developing responses to the following questions. Doing so will help you feel better prepared in meetings and will build confidence with your investors.

- What kind of companies are you investing in and why?
- Can you tell me about your investment philosophy?
- How do you plan to secure deal flow?
- Can you tell me about your past investment performance, personal or otherwise?
- Who are your lead investors?

6 Creating Legal Documents

Creating legal documents is a straightforward process. Unless you are an attorney, I do not recommend drafting your own legal documents - it's just too risky. I am also not an attorney, so this chapter focuses mainly on the basic set of documents you need as you get your fund off the ground. Such documents include the Private Placement Memorandum, Limited Partner Agreement, and the Subscription Agreement.

Private Placement Memorandum ✻

The Private Placement Memorandum (PPM) provides a high-level overview of what an investor needs to know about your fund. It contains information about who is managing the fund, the fund's investment focus, the purpose and investment strategy, and principal terms. Another important section in the PPM is the risk disclosures section. The risk disclosures section is a summary of most (but not all) of the common risks associated with investing in an early stage fund. While this list is not absolute, it must be disclosed.

Not all fund managers will create and issue a private placement memorandum. More often than not, managers avoid creating one because PPMs are perceived as cumbersome to create and unnecessary in light of having a robust and thorough limited partner agreement. There is no right or wrong here, so just use your judgment as to whether or not using a PPM is right for you.

Limited Partner Agreement

The limited partner agreement (LPA) describes all of the intricate details for how a fund operates. You may also hear the LPA referred to as an operating agreement, but they're basically the same thing. The LPA describes the formation of the partnership as a legal entity and describes its purpose. It contains basic information such as the legal place of business, the name and address of the limited partnership, and the term of the fund. It also contains more complex details such as how partners are admitted to the partnership, fund distributions, fund contributions, and GP/LP split.

The LPA also outlines the rights, powers, and limitations of the general partner when operating the fund and making investment decisions. The LP's rights and limitations are also described. Other important areas covered in the LPA describe how valuations, transfer of assets, taxes, capital calls, expenses, and management fees are handled. There are also details on what happens to the GP if they default on their commitment to the fund.

While the general partner has full discretionary authority over the investment portfolio, the LPs do have the right to remove the GP under certain circumstances. Removing the GP usually requires a sixty-six and two-thirds percent vote of the LPs. The LPs rights and limitations are also described.

The LPA also outlines the specifics for organizational costs. Organizational costs are defined as the initial start-up costs associated with organizing and establishing an investment fund. Such costs include, but are not limited to, travel, legal, administrative, marketing, equipment, I.T. services, and other expenses. Organizational costs vary in scope, but for a small fund under $10 million these initial, one-time costs can be anywhere from $25,000 to $75,000. For larger funds north of $100M, these costs can be anywhere from $250,000 to $800,000.

You should expect to pay for all of your travel and marketing expenses as these expenses are incurred. However, once your fund is up and running, you can gradually begin to reimburse yourself for these expenses. In your offering documents, you should indicate a maximum total amount for what you expect your organizational expenses to be. See example language below:

"The Fund will bear all expenses incident to the organization of the Fund, the General Partner and related entities (not to exceed "X" amount of dollars). In addition, the Fund shall also bear all costs incurred in connection with operation of its business, including those costs associated with holding or sale of securities; all legal, audit, registration, financial fees; the cost of Fund meetings, and any extraordinary expenses of the Fund."

Your attorney may word this differently, but this statement captures the essence of what such a statement looks and sounds like. In addition, your accountant will be able to choose the best method for recouping and reconciling fund formation costs.

Reimbursement of organizational costs is standard industry practice and will not be a point of contention with your LPs (unless you fail to set a maximum limit). As I stated previously, try to keep organizational costs as low as possible. The more dollars you can put into investing in the fund versus sunk organizational costs, the better.

The LPA is an important document that contains a wealth of information about the mechanics of your fund. As mentioned previously, the LPA is sometimes used in place of a private placement memorandum. If you are a new fund manager, relying solely on the LPA may be something you consider trying for your second fund, not your first.

Subscription Agreement

The Subscription Agreement describes the process for how limited partners purchase interest in (or subscribe to) a fund. It describes what each investor must agree to in the PPM and the LPA before they invest. The subscription agreement contains representations and warranties, certifying that each limited partner has reviewed and understands all of the offering documents and acknowledges that he/she is an accredited investor.

The PPM, LPA, and subscription agreement are the three core legal documents you will need at this point in the process. Before you pass off the creation of these documents to your attorney, think through the details of how you want to structure your fund and what provisions you'd like to include or exclude. It'll be a much smoother process answering questions from your attorney if you've thought through the details in advance.

Action Items

1. Read through a few example PPMs, LPAs, and subscription agreements to get a sense for how they're assembled and what sections they contain. As you read through the documents, take notes on what you like and don't like and share this with your attorney. *Note:* When I was in the research phase of the fund we started, I asked every fund manager I spoke with to send me their offering documents. Not all of them did, but I was

able to gather several sets of offering documents to use as examples to get started.

2. Obtain a few referrals for a securities attorney and set up some introductory interviews. Ideally, you should try to find someone with experience that can help you think through what you should and should not include in your legal documents.

3. Make a list of what you expect your upfront organizational costs will be. Include items such as marketing materials, travel, entertainment, website development, and legal and accounting expenses.

4. Spend some time with your team to develop an estimate for how long you think it will take to raise your fund. Having an estimated time-frame in mind is helpful for budgeting purposes. Your fundraising and marketing budget must be monitored closely.

7 Fund Reporting & Accounting Basics

As the general partner of an investment fund, you are not only responsible for investing in good companies but for managing the operational side of the fund as well. Ideally, you will have support staff that handles the accounting and reporting, but if you're just starting out you may not have the luxury of having an in-house team to perform these functions for you just yet. Even though you will not perform your own accounting and reporting, you still need to understand what it takes to create these documents on a quarterly basis.

At the most basic level quarterly reports typically contain the following sections:

#1 Fund Manager Commentary

One of my favorite sections of the quarterly report is the fund manager's commentary. This is normally the first section in the report and is helpful for gaining insight and perspective into what is top-of-mind to the fund manager. It's in this section where the fund manager may share her perspective on a particular industry vertical or she may talk about why certain companies were added to the portfolio. The number of topics can vary greatly. As most fund managers are unable to regularly speak to their investors, the management commentary gives them an opportunity to communicate at high-level how things have been going at the fund.

As you begin to think through what you'd like to communicate to your investors in this section, keep your writing factual and objective, but personal at the same time. LPs expect GPs to highlight things that are going well, but it's perfectly okay to point out things that aren't going so well. For example, maybe one of your prominent portfolio companies had a valuation mark down - talk about why. Transparency with your investors goes a long way. I have learned from experience that investors would rather hear bad news than no news at all. I once worked with a start-up tech company that only communicated with its investors when they needed money. As a result, the investors were reluctant to re-up on their investment and the company struggled to raise the capital that it desperately needed.

I'm by no means implying that within the manager's commentary section you should *only* share bad news with your investors. That makes no sense. I'm only trying to emphasize that you should keep your commentary balanced, objective, and transparent. Your investors will appreciate that.

As much as you can you should by no means ever make absolute statements about performance unless you are 100% certain it will happen (like a company exit, for example). The manager's commentary isn't about inflating your investor's hopes: it's an area where you have the opportunity to expound on your investment strategy and explain how you are adapting and taking advantage of opportunities in the market. If you think it's additive to discuss a poor investment decision, you should also include your plan for how you will use what you learned to make positive changes to the portfolio in the future.

#2 Performance

Financial performance should be included in the quarterly report. Basic information to includes is total committed capital, capital called to date, total LP contributions, total number of portfolio company investments, total distributions, total LP distributions, total value of remaining companies, and the total number of active companies remaining in the portfolio.

We briefly touched on the following performance metrics in Chapter 5, but I'll provide a little more depth on the other performance metrics that should be included in the quarterly report.

Total Value to Paid-in Capital

Total Value to Paid-in Capital (TVPI) is calculated as the total market value of all the companies in the portfolio plus total LP distributions, divided by the total amount of money paid into the fund. TVPI is used to demonstrate the increase (or decrease) in intrinsic value of the fund (even if you haven't paid any distributions to LPs).

For private companies, valuations are measured by a third-party using the Financial Accounting Standards Board's (FASB), Accounting Standards Codification 820, Level 3 Fair Value Measurement guidelines. The FASB 820 guideline establishes a fair value hierarchy that prioritizes the inputs to valuation techniques used to measure fair value. Level 3 assets are illiquid assets having unobservable inputs. Unobservable inputs are used to measure fair value to the extent that relevant observable inputs are not available, thereby allowing for situations in which there is little, if any, market activity for the asset at the measurement date. **However, the fair value measurement objective remains the same, that is, an exit price from the perspective of a market participant that**

holds the asset. Therefore, unobservable inputs will reflect the reporting entity's own assumptions about the assumptions that market participants would use in pricing the asset (including assumptions about risk). Unobservable inputs should be developed based on the best information available in the circumstances, which might include the reporting entity's own data [1].

Internal Rate of Return

Internal Rate of Return (IRR) is a discount rate that makes the net present value (NPV) of all cash flows from a particular project equal to zero. IRR is commonly used to compare VC fund returns to public market returns, or the public market equivalent. The Public Market Equivalent, or PME, is the public market rate of return as compared to a VC fund's rate of return over the same time period. PME is easy to understand, however calculating it can sometimes be tricky. If you'd like further background on PME, please see the glossary towards the end of the book.

74

Distributions to Paid-in Capital

Distributions to Paid-in Capital (DPI) is the one metric that provides a measurement of the total amount of money distributed to investors. DPI is a ratio of total distributions to total paid in capital. A DPI less than 100% means the fund has not returned total invested capital to LPs. One of the drawbacks of looking solely at DPI to assess performance is that it does not take into account the increase in value of the underlying portfolio companies; it's only a measurement of distributions. As such, DPI should not be used early on in the life of a fund to determine how a fund will ultimately perform.

☆*Make sure you are comfortable with explaining this concept to your LPs because they are likely to ask about it.*

Residual Value to Paid-in Capital

Residual Value to Paid-in Capital (RVPI) is a ratio of the total market value remaining in a fund compared to total paid-in capital. This metric becomes more important towards the end of a fund's life than at the beginning because it provides an indication of how much value could still be paid out to investors from the remaining companies in the portfolio. I haven't seen many fund managers list this metric and for good reason. Having a large RVPI value remaining towards the tail-end of a fund's life suggests two things: 1). The fund may still realize the value and distribute cash to investors, or 2). the remaining value may never be realized. RVPI is not a widely used performance metric and there's nothing wrong with including in your quarterly reports if you feel it's necessary.

Portfolio Company Updates

Portfolio company updates should include a short description of what each company does and any notable milestones or achievements the company has made since the last quarterly report. If there is nothing important to report, then a full detailed summary on each company isn't necessary. As more companies are added to the portfolio, the length of each company update should be reduced to include the most important updates.

Other basic information to include (ideally in a table format) is name and description of the company, location, percent owned, date of initial investment, exit date, total capital invested, current cost, realized proceeds, and carrying value.

Financial Reporting

Within in 45 days after the close of each quarter you must provide each of your limited partners with a financial summary of the fund. To effectively do so, you will need (at a minimum) the following:

- Financial Statement
    - Income Statement
    - Balance Sheet
    - Cash Flow Statement
- Summary of Performance Metrics
    - TVPI, IRR, DPI
- Portfolio Company Valuations
- Investment Activity for the Quarter

Yes, producing all of these reports may seem overwhelming. It's best to outsource the reporting process or hire someone in-house to do it for you so for the following reasons:

1. Performance reports need to be delivered to LPs on time.

    a. Your limited partner agreement (LPA) will outline how many days you have after each quarter to provide financial statements to your LPs (it's usually forty-five, sixty, or ninety days).

2. Your financial and performance statements need to be correct.

Having operational support will make it easier for you to focus on the one thing that matters most – sourcing, investing, and building profitable companies. If you can't afford to hire in-house help, there are several third-party options for outsourcing this function.

Action Items

1. Make an outline of the items you'd like to include in your quarterly reports to investors. The financial statements and company reports should be included by default, but other helpful items may include a "manager's opinion" or "team update." Get creative and make it personable, but professional.

2. Find an accountant to help you set up your financials. Your accountant can be someone your hire in-house or it can be a third party. Interview several people/firms to find the best accounting services for your needs.

8 Setting Expectations

Investors who are unfamiliar with the nature of venture investing may initially have a hard time understanding the uneven pacing of returns and how they are distributed over time. It's incumbent upon you to set expectations early on so LPs understand the characteristics of venture investing and aren't surprised when they see some companies in your fund that failed to perform.

For the majority of VC funds, the Pareto Principle applies: The bulk of returns are derived from a handful of companies. And the companies that do perform well usually take longer to come to fruition. The companies that fail, fail early and fast. As such, one concept that may be helpful to explain to LPs is the concept of the J-Curve. The J-Curve is a graphical representation of investment performance that dips in the early years before gradually rising in later years, forming the letter "J" when plotted on a chart. As you see in the chart below, the curve gradually dips below the x-axis on the graph, and over time, slowly begins to rise into positive category before leveling off.

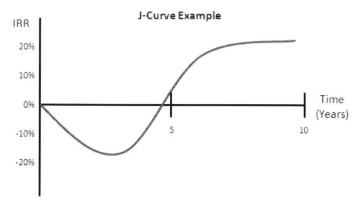

Source: http://sophisticatedinvestor.com/private-equity-and-the-j-curve/

Most all venture capital funds' performance will resemble the J-Curve for an extended period of time before crossing over into positive territory. The next logical question one might ask is, "why does this happen and how long does it usually take to get into positive territory?" As stated earlier, poorer investments fail early and fast. However, the twenty percent of companies that drive your returns are likely to take several years to mature and yield the return you and your investors desire.

Performance Expectations

Generally speaking, it's reasonable to expect early-stage venture investment returns to be in the range of 3x to 5x (sometimes higher) and later-stage venture investments to return 2x to 3x. The wide variance in performance is a function of risk vs. reward. The more risk investors take, invariably, the more reward they expect. Categorically, venture investing falls into the high-risk category. Therefore, it is almost always the smallest portion of an investment portfolio, with allocations to the sector ranging anywhere from 2% to 10% of a portfolio. Albeit the smallest allocation, venture has the widest dispersion of returns that are often uncorrelated to other investments in an investment portfolio.

Qualified Investors

Each investor in your fund will need to fill out an investor questionnaire that validates him or her as an accredited investor or qualified person. It is assumed that accredited and qualified investors are sophisticated enough to understand the risky nature of venture investing, but it never hurts to go the extra mile to make sure there is 100% clarity on the risk an investor is taking.

Setting clear expectations with LPs starts with being transparent about your investment strategy and educating them about the risk they're taking by investing in your fund. Investing in VC is a marathon, not a sprint. As such, it's important to help LPs understand the long-term nature of venture and that unlocking and delivering value happens slowly over time.

Action Items

1. Think through how you plan to set expectations with your investors. Is your

fund early or late stage? What is a realistic investment multiple for the industry you're investing in? How often will you make distributions? How frequent will you send out communications about the fund? Etc.

9 Building a Winning Team

Starting an investment fund from scratch is difficult and it's even harder to do alone. As such, the next topic I'd like to cover is the people you will need in order to get it done.

The investment team leads and makes all investment decisions for the fund. The investment team is usually made up of the general partners and/or partners of a firm. The members of the investment team should be carefully selected. However, if you plan to start out as a one-person shop, then assembling a team will not immediately apply to you. But team dynamics and makeup will come to the fore as your fund grows in the future.

Working on a team makes it easier to collaborate on new ideas and have additional perspectives when making investment decisions.

One-person investment funds are not the norm but are not uncommon either. However, one problem with one-person investment funds is confirmation bias. Confirmation bias is the tendency to process and analyze information in such a way that it supports one's preexisting ideas and convictions. Most people try hard to avoid falling victim to confirmation bias. Confirmation bias is much less of a problem when there is more than one person involved in the decision-making process.

Group-Think

Working on a team is great, but more often than not group-think (which is in essence is confirmation bias shared between two or more people) can become a problem if there are no checks and balances to control it. It is best to construct a team comprised of people with backgrounds different but complementary to your own, so you don't fall into the trap of confirmation bias or group-think.

Paul Gompers, professor at Harvard Business School, and two of his research associates (Kevin

Huang and Sophie Wang) authored a paper titled "Homophile in Entrepreneurial Team Formation." (RP) In the paper, they highlight the causal relationship between team diversity and performance. Heterogeneous teams benefit from more diverse pools of skill and knowledge, but at the same time, differences in ethnicity, culture, and mother language hinder efficient communication among team members, thus potentially lowering productivity [1]. Another result of their analysis showed that when participants in the study were allowed to choose their own teams to start a microbusiness, the propensity to pair up was increased by common personal characteristics including ethnicity, gender, education, and work experience [2]." In the end, the purpose of the paper was to acknowledge and discuss the drivers that affect organizational diversity and how it impacts entrepreneurial team formation and the venture capital industry. Understanding the subtle dynamics of teams will greatly help you as you assemble the team that will eventually help you manage your fund.

As investors assess your fund, you will need to help them get a sense of how well you and your team work together. Highlight how you and your partners came to know each other and why you chose to team up on the fund. Describe a few projects you've worked on and how you've gotten to know each other's working style. It's beneficial to tell investors how you see your team growing in the future and what the team structure looks like as your fund grows. Effectively articulating future growth plans instills confidence in your investors that you plan to stick around for the long-term.

Advisors

As you build out your team give careful thought to whether and how soon you should add advisors and/or venture partners to your organization. Advisors can be used in a variety of ways from providing advice about portfolio companies or making introductions to potential investors. A strong array of advisors will include individuals with specific industry expertise such as enterprise software or biotech, for example. The objective of having advisors involved is to expand the scope of advice and connections you are able to offer your portfolio companies and to help you in areas where you may not have as much experience. It is not uncommon for advisors to receive some form of compensation, which usually comes in the form of a small percent of the carry of the fund. The amount paid to advisors varies from fund-to-fund. Advisors do not make investment decisions and are not involved in day-to-day operations of the fund. Keep in mind, that the subject matter expert advisors we are discussing here are distinct and separate from LPs that may serve on a fund's advisory board. An LP advisory board provides governance and policy expertise for the fund and nothing more. As such, they are not liable for any actions taken by the fund.

Venture Partners — *Ibec w/ Bob*

Venture partners can be greatly additive to a venture capital fund. While venture partners are not members of the investment team, they do wield influence. Their primary duties involve sourcing new opportunities and working closely with portfolio companies. Venture partners often serve in key operational roles at startup companies and are compensated to do so. According to Boris Wentz at VersionOne VC, "venture partners are usually seasoned entrepreneurs and executives that have a deep understanding of a particular industry and how to run a company within that industry [3]." They are not full members of the management team and they may not stay affiliated with a firm indefinitely. However, the value they add is invaluable as they can help jumpstart a company's momentum and get it closer to achieving its goals faster than it could on its own.

Action Items

1. Make a list of industry and subject matter experts that could serve as advisors or venture partners for your fund.

2. Define in advance your expectations for advisors and don't just add names to your list (or website) for window dressing purposes.

10 Putting it all Together

Throughout the fundraising process it's good
practice to regularly take a step back from the
process and remember that with each person you
meet you're building a relationship. Many prospects
you approach may not invest with you the first time
around. However, you still want to make a good
impression so that they are open to having you back
for a discussion when you're raising your next fund.
Those who do decide to invest in you are in a way
becoming part of your team and are an essential
part of your journey. Making a 10-year commitment
to invest in a first-time venture capital fund is no
small decision. It takes faith and patience. As such,
you should seek to build a strong relationship with
each of your investors because the relationships
you build will outlast any fund you start.

Some of the best ways to nurture your relationships are to maintain a culture of openness, regular communication, and by delivering strong performance. Doing these things consistently will help your investors gain confidence in you and your team's ability to create a meaningful investment fund.

Closing Words

Whether you're just starting out in venture, or you've been in the business for a long time, raising money is difficult. Doing so successfully requires patience, persistence, and the ability to build enduring and trusting relationships. It's reasonable to expect a lot of people to tell you "no," and that's okay. Kleiner Perkins, one of the Silicon Valley's most successful VC funds, raised just $7.5 million for its first fund. Granted this was in 1972 but nevertheless, it was comparatively a small amount of money, even back then. Since then, Kleiner Perkins has gone on to perform exceptionally well having raised over $10B in assets across 20 venture funds. Whether or not you become the next Kleiner Perkins, that's for you to determine. As with most things in venture, there are no certainties. But one thing is certain, if you don't start somewhere, you'll never know what the outcome might be.

Acknowledgments

My wife, Rachel, has been my biggest supporter, not only for this book, but in everything I've ever sought to do personally and professionally. Blake Trippet, who has been a great friend and confidant, provided wonderful feedback on this book and I am thankful for his knowledge and perspective. Drew Ramsey, thank you for your support and expertise in marketing, and Romain David who was instrumental in helping me understand the nuances of writing and working with designers and editors. Samantha Hanni, thank you for editing the very first version of this book. Your feedback on how to put this book together was extremely helpful. And lastly, I thank God for all the opportunities I've been given that helped provide the background for this book. I am truly blessed.

About the Author

Kevin Moore is a partner at Spur Capital Partners and has over 11 years of experience in the financial industry. Prior to Spur, Kevin was the Director of Angel Investments at i2E, an early-stage, venture investment firm. At i2E, Kevin advised and invested in early-stage, startup technology companies and also played an instrumental role in the creation of i2E's first privately-funded investment fund. For the past three years, Kevin has served as a Governor-appointed Trustee on the Investment Committee for the Oklahoma Teacher's Retirement System Board of Trustees, a $16B pension fund. Kevin received a Bachelor of Science in civil engineering from Oklahoma State University and an MBA from the University of Central Oklahoma. Kevin resides in Oklahoma City with his wife, Rachel, and children, Taylor and Isaac.

Glossary

Advisory Board – A board of limited partners appointed by the general partners to perform a variety of duties for a particular limited partnership. Common duties include addressing conflicts of interest, approving valuation methods and approving mark-ups and mark-downs.

Angel Investor - an affluent individual who provides capital for a business start-up, usually in exchange for convertible debt or ownership equity.

Capital Account – Account established for each partner reflecting value of initial capital contributions, profits assigned to the account, losses assigned to the account, and withdrawals by the partner.

Capital Calls - are issued to limited partners when the general partner has identified a new investment and a portion of the limited partner's committed capital is required to pay for that investment.

Carried Interest - Carried interest is a share of any profits that the general partners of private equity and hedge funds receive as compensation, regardless of whether or not they contributed any initial funds. This method of compensation seeks to motivate the general partner (fund manager) to work toward improving the fund's performance. Carried interest usually ranges between five and thirty percent.

Clawback provision - gives the limited partners the right to reclaim a portion of the general partner's carried interest in the event that losses from later investments cause the general partner to withhold too much carried interest.

Co-Investment Rights – A contractual obligation to offer one or more investors the chance to invest additional equity alongside of a deal sponsor.

Committed Capital - Money that is committed by limited partners to a fund. It is usually not invested immediately. It is "drawn down" and invested over time as investments are identified.

Cumulative Distributions - or the total amount of cash and stock that has been paid out to the limited partners.

Fund Capitalization – The total amount of capital committed to a fund by the LPs or investors.

Fund Size – The total amount of capital committed by the limited and general partners of a fund.

Fund Term – The period of time, contractually established by a partnership agreement, during which the general partner can make and harvest investments.

Fund-of-funds – A fund that takes limited partnership interests in other private equity or venture capital funds.

General Partners - are responsible for managing the investments within the private equity fund. For their services, they earn a management fee and a percentage of the fund's profits, called carried interest. The general partners can be legally liable for the actions of the fund.

GP Clawback – An obligation of the general partner to protect the 80-20 profit split (typically) and promised priority return established by the partnership agreement.

Internal Rate of Return - the fund's IRR since inception, or "SI-IRR", is a common formula that potential private equity investors should be able to recognize. It is simply the fund's internal rate of return since its first investment.

GP Contribution – The money invested by the general partner in its own fund.

Investment Period – The period of time in which the general partner can add new portfolio companies to the fund at its own discretion.

Limited partners - are usually institutional or high net worth investors interested in receiving the income and capital gains associated with investing in the private equity fund. Limited partners do not take part in the fund's active management. They are protected from losses beyond their original investment as well as any legal actions taken against the fund.

LP Clawback – An obligation of limited partners to return prior distributions to cover legal judgments and other liabilities of the general partner.

Management Fee – Annual fee paid by the limited partners to the general partner to cover such expenses as salaries, bonuses, office rents, and other expenses related to the operation of the partnership not covered by the fund.

Most Favored Nation Clause – Provision in a partnership agreement giving investors the ability to see unique terms and conditions offered to other investors in side letters and to obtain the same terms and conditions.

No-Fault Divorce Clause – A provision in a partnership agreement that allows the limited partners, upon a majority or higher vote, to suspend the investment period of the fund for any reason.

No-fault Suspension – A provision in a partnership agreement that allows the limited partners, upon a majority of higher vote, to suspend the investment period of the fund for any reason.

Organization Expenses – Expenses having to do with the formation of a limited partnership.

Paid-in Capital - is the cumulative amount of capital that has been drawn down. The amount of paid-in capital that has actually been invested into the fund's portfolio companies is simply referred to as invested capital.

Paid-in Capital Multiple is calculated by dividing paid-in capital by committed capital. This ratio shows a potential investor the percentage of a fund's committed capital that has actually been drawn down. (**PIC Multiple = Paid-in Capital/Committed Capital**)

Placement Agent – Third-party broker dealer hired by private equity firms to help market their funds to prospective investors.

Portfolio Company - The company or entity into which a fund invests directly.

Preferred or Priority return – Distributions made to limited partners to ensure they receive a certain annual return on their money – often 8 percent – before the general partner shares in profit distributions.

Public Market Equivalent (PME) designs a set of analyses used in the Private Equity Industry to evaluate the performance of a Private Equity Fund against a public benchmark or index. The PME calculation discounts (or invests) all cash contributions to, and any residual value of, the fund at the public market total return and divides the resulting value by the value of all cash contributions discounted (or invested) at the public market total return. The PME can be viewed as a market-adjusted multiple of invested capital (net of fees). The PME can be viewed as a market-adjusted multiple of invested capital net of fees. A PME of 1.30, for example, implies that at the end of the fund's life, investors ended up with 30% more than they would have if they had invested in the public markets [1].

Realization Multiple is also known as the distributions to paid-in (DPI) multiple. It is calculated by dividing the cumulative distributions by paid-in capital. The realization multiple, in conjunction with the investment multiple, gives a potential private equity investor insight into how much of the fund's return has actually been "realized", or paid out, to investors. **(DPI = Cumulative Distributions/Paid-in Capital)**

Recycling Provisions – Clauses in partnership agreements allowing the general partner to re-invest distributions from prior realizations in new investments.

Residual value is the market value of the remaining equity that the limited partners have in the fund.

Residual Value to Paid in Multiple (RVPI) is calculated by dividing the fund's residual value by paid-in capital. It provides a measurement, in conjunction with the investment multiple, of how much of the fund's return is unrealized and dependent on the market value of its investments. **(RVPI = Residual Value/Paid-in Capital)**

Side Letter – Contract signed between the general partner and a particular limited partner giving that limited partner terms and conditions that are different from the main limited partnership agreement.

Terms and Conditions – The financial and management conditions under which private equity limited partnerships are structured.

Total Value to Paid-in Multiple (TVPI) is also known as the investment multiple. It is calculated by dividing the fund's cumulative distributions and residual value by the paid-in capital. It gives a potential investor insight into the fund's performance by showing the fund's total value as a multiple of its cost basis. It does not take into account the time value of money. **(TVPI = (Cumulative Distributions + Residual Value)/Paid-in Capital)**

Transaction Fees – Fees that a general partner charges its portfolio companies upon the successful completion of a transaction, such as the acquisition or sale of the portfolio companies.

The Global Investment Performance Standards (GIPS) - require that the following ratios be present when private equity firms present their performance to prospective investors.

Unrelated Business Taxable Income – Income that tax-exempt organizations do have to pay taxes on because it is not sufficiently related to the purpose of the tax-exempt organization.

Valuation Method – The policy guidelines a management team uses to value the holdings in the fund's portfolio.

Venture Capital - Venture capital is financing that investors provide to startup companies and small businesses that are believed to have long-term growth potential. Venture capital generally comes from well-off investors, investment banks and many other financial institutions.

Vintage Year - The first year that the private equity fund draws down or "calls" committed capital.

Write-down – A reduction in the value of an investment.

Write-off – The write-down of a portfolio company's holdings to a valuation of zero.

Write-up – An increase in the value of an investment.

110

References

Chapter 4

[1]   Preqin Special Report: Up & Away: Launching A First-Time Venture Capital Fund, 2017

Chapter 5

[1]   https://mattermark.com/the-micro-vcs-are-coming/
[2]   http://www.cambridgeassociates.com/wp-content/uploads/2015/11/Venture-Capital-Disrupts-Venture-Capital.pdf

Chapter 7

[1]   www.fasb.org

Chapter 9

[1]   Alesina, A., & Ferrara, E. L. (2005). Ethnic diversity and economic performance. Journal of economic literature, 43(3), 762-800.
[2]   Gompers, P., Huang, K., Wang, S. (2017). Homophile in Entrepreneurial Team Formation. Harvard Business School, Working Paper 17-104
[3]   http://versionone.vc/what-does-a-venture-partner-do/#ixzz517CsbjMX

Glossary

[1]   Financial Intermediation in private equity: How well do fund of funds perform. Harris, Jenkinson, Kaplan and Stucke (2017)

Helpful Reading

Raising Venture Capital for the Serious Entrepreneur
by Dermot Berkery

Mastering the VC Game
by Jeff Bussgang

The Money of Invention
by Paul Gompers and Josh Lerner

The Startup Game
by William H. Draper III

The Venture Capital Cycle
by Paul Gompers and Josh Lerner

The Creator's Code
by Amy Wilkinson

The Intelligent Entrepreneur
by Bill Murphy Jr

Business Valuation
by David Perkins

The Rainforest
by Victor Hwang and Greg Horowitt

64855347R00066

Made in the USA
Middletown, DE
18 February 2018